SOLVING SCIENCE MYSTERIES

Why Do Glaciers Grind?

All About Extreme Environments

Helen Bethune

PowerKiDS press.

New York

Published in 2010 by The Rosen Publishing Group, Inc.
29 East 21st Street, New York, NY 10010

Produced and designed by Denise Ryan & Associates
Editor: Helen Moore and Edwina Hamilton
Designer: Anita Adams
Photographer: Lyz Turner-Clark
U.S. Editor: Kara Murray

Photo Credits: p. 4 banner and bottom: Izabela Keppler; p. 4 middle left: Diane Miller; p. 5 top banner: Mischa van Lieshout; p. 5 top right: Roman Krochuk; p. 5 second from top: James Steidl; p. 5 third from top: © Photographer: Grauzikas | Agency: Dreamstime.com; p. 5 bottom: © Photographer: Dean Perrus | Agency: Dreamstime.com; p. 5 bottom left: © Photographer: Dennis Sabo | Agency: Dreamstime.com; p. 6 top: Jan Will; p. 6 top left: Alexander Hafemann; p. 7 top: Sherwood Imagery; p. 7 bottom left: John Pitcher; p. 7 bottom middle: © Photographer: Gail Johnson | Agency: Dreamstime.com; pp. 7 bottom right and 16 bottom: arcticphoto.co.uk; p. 8 middle: © Photographer: Lori Howard | Agency: Dreamstime.com; p. 8 bottom: © Karen Graham | Dreamstime.com; p. 9 top: © Photographer: Maunger | Agency: Dreamstime.com; p. 9 bottom: © Photographer: Jessica Bethke | Agency: Dreamstime.com; pp. 10 bottom left, 11 right, 12 top, 13 bottom: Photolibrary; p. 10 bottom right: © Photographer: Abstractx | Agency: Dreamstime.com; p. 11 bottom: © Photographer: Marco Regalia | Agency: Dreamstime.com; p. 12 middle left (map of Jamaica credit): Pawel Gaul; p. 12 bottom right: Pat Watt and Bill Dillon; p. 13 top: NOAA; p. 15 top and middle: NASA; p. 15 bottom: © Photographer: Fred Goldstein | Agency: Dreamstime.com; p. 16 Photolibrary; p. 17 top: Photo Courtesy of Professor Matthew England; p. 17 bottom: © Armin Rose | Dreamstime.com p. 19: AAP Images.

Library of Congress Cataloging-in-Publication Data

Bethune, Helen.
    Why do glaciers grind? : all about extreme environments / Helen Bethune.
        p. cm. — (Solving science mysteries)
    Includes index.
    ISBN 978-1-4488-0391-0 (library binding) — ISBN 978-1-4488-0392-7 (pbk.) —
ISBN 978-1-4488-0393-4 (6-pack)
    1. Climatology—Juvenile literature. 2. Extreme environments—Juvenile literature. 3. Glaciers—Juvenile literature.
I. Title.
    QC863.5.B48 2010
    551.31'2—dc22

                                        2009038269

Manufactured in the United States of America

CPSIA Compliance Information: Batch #WW10PK: For Further Information contact Rosen Publishing, New York, New York at 1-800-237-9932

Contents

Questions About Extreme Environments

Q: What is an extreme environment?

A: An extreme environment is a place where the conditions require a great amount of adaptation for survival. People and living things need certain levels of air pressure, temperature, radiation, dryness, and oxygen to exist without physical hardship.

Q: Where are extreme environments?

A: Extreme environments are located at Earth's polar regions—the Arctic and Antarctica—high altitudes, as well as deep under ground, and in deserts, oceans, and outer space. Climate and changes in climate can cause extreme environments, too. The weather can cause extreme environments. Blizzards, ice storms, and droughts all create extreme living conditions for people, plants, and animals.

Q: What are some other examples of extreme environments on Earth?

A: Some places on Earth, such as the **tundra**, glaciers, volcanoes, caves, oceans, and swamps, are environmental extremes. The people, plants, and animals that live there must develop special ways of adjusting to the conditions to be able to survive.

In most cases, environments are extreme because of where they are on Earth's surface. For instance, temperatures in the depths of the ocean are very, very cold whereas swamps in the tropics, close to the equator, are hot and **humid** for most of the year.

Questions About Extreme Climates

Q: Do deserts have extreme climates?

A: Yes, deserts do have extreme climates. They are dry regions, which usually receive less than 10 inches (25 cm) of **precipitation** a year. The world's deserts are divided into four categories.

Subtropical deserts are the hottest, with parched **terrain** and rapid evaporation. Cool coastal deserts are located within the same **latitudes** as subtropical deserts, but the average temperature is not as hot because of cold offshore ocean currents. Cold winter deserts are marked by temperature differences, ranging from 100° F (38° C) in summer to 10° F (−12° C) in winter. Polar regions are also deserts because nearly all the moisture in these areas is locked up in the form of ice.

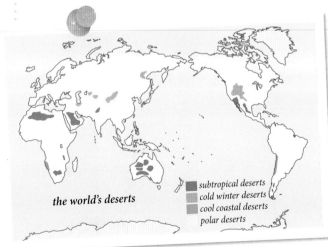

the world's deserts

■ subtropical deserts
■ cold winter deserts
■ cool coastal deserts
■ polar deserts

Q: Do people live in the polar regions?

A: Yes, approximately four million people live in the Arctic regions, as well as many types of animals and plant life. Most of the Arctic is an ocean covered by a 10-foot (3 m) sheet of ice that is surrounded by land.

Most people who go to Antarctica are scientists who conduct experiments on life in such conditions. They do not live there permanently. Only penguins and sea creatures survive naturally in the southern polar region. Antarctica is a **continent**, just like North America or Europe, however it is covered by thousands of feet (m) of ice and snow.

The Arctic Inuits

The Inuits of Canada and Greenland were hunters and gatherers. They hunted herds of caribou for meat and fur for warm clothing. They also gathered berries, seaweed, and eggs for food.

Today, the Inuit way of life is very different. They have developed economic programs, including running airlines, offshore and high seas fisheries, ecological and cultural tourism, selling Arctic foods, marine transportation, hunting and fishing trips for non-Inuits, and real estate. All these pursuits take into account the extreme environment in which they live.

Questions About Extreme Weather

Q: What causes floods?

A: Floods occur when rivers, streams, or drains overflow. The excess water spills over the banks and floods the surrounding areas. Floods are usually caused by intense local rainfall, snowmelt, or a combination of both. A heavy downpour from hurricanes or other tropical storms can also cause serious flooding.

Floods are one of nature's most dangerous natural hazards. In some places, they are frequent and can happen rapidly and unexpectedly. They often affect large areas, causing widespread loss of life and property.

Q: What is the difference between a blizzard and an ice storm?

A: A blizzard is a massive snowstorm with heavy winds of up to 25 miles per hour (40 km/h) or more, making it very hard to see. The **windchill** is dangerous as it can be –13° F (–25° C) or less. These conditions must last for 4 hours or more to be officially classified as a blizzard. Blizzards can cause enormous damage, blocking roads and highways, and burying everything in snow.

An ice storm happens when rain falls onto a surface with a temperature below freezing. This causes it to freeze to surfaces, such as trees, cars and roads, forming a coating or glaze of ice. Ice is heavy and it can bring down trees and communication lines and towers.

Questions About Extraordinary Extremes

Q: Why do glaciers grind?

A: Glaciers are bodies of ice and snow that remain solid all year round. They form when more snow falls each winter than melts each summer. Ice is very heavy and begins to move downhill, under the force of gravity. High pressure causes the ice to wrap around rocks, gravel, and boulders. These are carried downhill along with the glacial ice. Over thousands of years, the weight of rock and ice in the glacier grinding together makes deep gouges in the rocky slopes. They can carve **cirques**, **spurs**, mountain lakes, hanging valleys, and create lakes. Glaciers can move mountains!

cirque formed by glacial erosion

spur formed by glacial erosion

Q: Why do volcanoes erupt?

A: Volcanoes erupt when the rock inside our planet becomes too hot and melts to become **magma**. Magma is less dense than the surrounding rock, so it rises to the surface and escapes through a vent, or volcano. The magma often contains water and dissolved gases so when it reaches the surface, the mixture suddenly expands into steam and gas, causing a violent eruption.

Vulcanologists use very sophisticated instruments to measure a volcano's movement and the amount of gas it is producing. They do this to establish whether it is going to erupt, so they can warn people in plenty of time and tell them to evacuate the area.

It's a fact

tree house, New Guinea

> Jamaican Tremors

Scientists believe that a serious earthquake in Jamaica is long overdue because the country has not had a major earthquake for over 100 years. Jamaica experiences about 200 earthquakes each year, but the last major earthquake occurred in 1907.

> Swamp Life

The Kombai people live in tree houses in the swampy interior of New Guinea. The height provides the inhabitants with cool breezes. Their dwellings are between 33 and 115 feet (10–35 m) above the ground.

> Raincoats Required

Mount Waialeale on the island of Kauai, Hawaii, is the rainiest place on Earth. It rains for more than 335 days every year!

Mount Waialeale, Hawaii

> Life in the Depths

At the ocean's deepest point, the Mariana Trench, in the western Pacific Ocean, the water pressure is the equivalent of having about 50 jumbo jets on top of you. Yet, even here life thrives nearly 7 miles (11 km) below the surface of the ocean. Scientists have found that the seafloor holds soft-walled, single-cell organisms that are thought to resemble some of the world's earliest life-forms.

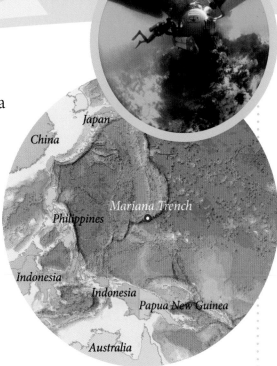

> Shifting Sands

Because of the **deforestation** of the woodlands in northern China, over 1 million tons (1 million t) of sand blows into Beijing from the Gobi Desert each year. The sand makes the sky look yellow. There are now sand dunes as close as 49 miles (79 km) to Beijing, with estimates that these are drifting closer at a rate of 2 miles (3 km) a year.

Can You Believe It?

Global Warming

Our climate is changing. Glaciers are melting, droughts are lasting longer, and extreme weather events such as fires, floods, and tornadoes are occurring more often. Many scientists believe that global warming causes such extremes.

Global warming is an increase in the average temperature of Earth's atmosphere. Earth's atmosphere contains not only air but also a mixture of gases that help support life on our planet. These gases are called greenhouse gases. However, our use of **fossil fuels** is releasing too much carbon dioxide into the atmosphere, making the planet warmer than it would be without human activity. Nobody knew how harmful this was for a long time, but now we know we have to care for our planet by recycling and using our cars less.

Greenhouse Gases

Just like in a greenhouse, greenhouses gases trap the Sun's heat and keep heat from going into space. This is a natural effect. If this did not happen, Earth would be quite cold

Some energy is reflected into space.

Earth's surface is heated by the Sun and radiates the heat toward space.

Solar energy from the Sun passes through the atmosphere.

Greenhouse gases in the atmosphere trap some of the heat.

Events of Great Magnitude

An earthquake that struck Chile on May 22, 1960, had a **magnitude** of 9.5 on the Richter scale. It was the strongest earthquake ever recorded. The second-strongest earthquake in the world occurred on December 26, 2004. It had a magnitude of 9.3 and caused a deadly tsunami in the Indian Ocean.

Greenland's Melting Glaciers

Scientists have evidence that Greenland's glaciers are sliding toward the sea much faster than previously believed. They had thought that the entire Greenland ice sheet could melt in about 1,000 years, but it may be much sooner. This means that sea levels will rise faster as well. If the Greenland ice sheet melted completely, it would raise global sea levels by about 23 feet (7 m).

Who Found out?

The Mighty Mississippi: Jacques Marquette

French-born priest Father Jacques Marquette (1637–1675) was one of the first Europeans to explore the Mississippi River. Seven years after he arrived in New France (Canada, Acadia, Louisiana, and Newfoundland), he accompanied Louis Joliet on an expedition to find the large river that was rumored to be in the south. The French hoped this river would lead them to the Pacific Ocean.

In 1673, Joliet, Marquette, and five other men began their expedition by following Lake Michigan to Green Bay. They canoed up the Fox River, crossed over to the Wisconsin, and followed that river downstream to the Mississippi. The further south they went, the more convinced they became that the Mississippi flowed into the Gulf of Mexico and not the Pacific as they had hoped. When the men realized that they may be in danger from the Spanish and tribes hostile to the French, they returned to Lake Michigan with the help of the Illini tribe.

Climate Change:
Professor Matthew England

The Sydney-born professor Matthew England (1966–), a physical **oceanographer** and **climatologist**, has determined the influence of climate change on the Southern Ocean and regional weather patterns, especially with regard to the rainfall decline across southern Australia. Professor England's research on what controls ocean currents and how these currents affect climate has made him world renowned. In 2007, he led a major declaration by scientists at the United Nations Climate Change Conference held in Bali, Indonesia. He is currently an Australian Research Council Federation Fellow and codirector of the Climate Change Research Centre at the University of New South Wales.

The Bathysphere:
William Beebe and Otis Barton

The bathysphere was invented by Americans William Beebe (1877–1962) and Otis Barton (1899–1992) around 1930. A bathysphere is a pressurized metal sphere that allows people to go to depths in the ocean at which diving unaided is impossible. This hollow cast-iron sphere with very thick walls is lowered and raised from a ship using a steel cable. William Beebe tested a 4.8 feet (1.45 m) in diameter bathysphere in 1930, going down to 1,427 feet (435 m). Beebe and Barton descended about 3,000 feet (914 m) in a larger bathysphere in 1934 off the coast of Nonsuch Island, Bermuda, in the Atlantic Ocean. During the dive, they communicated with the surface by telephone.

First Conquerors of Mount Everest: Edmund Hillary and Tenzing Norgay

The first people to reach the summit of Mount Everest, the highest mountain peak in the world, were Edmund Hillary, a former beekeeper from New Zealand, and Tenzing Norgay, a Sherpa climber from Nepal. Mount Everest is 29,035 feet (8,850 m) high and is in Tibet. Temperatures at the top of Mount Everest can fall as low as −76° F (− 60° C). Even in July, the warmest month, the average temperature is only −2° F (−19° C). Ten camps had to be established along the route to enable the climbing team to overcome the effects of altitude. Hillary and Tenzing made their successful attempt on the peak itself on May 29, 1953.

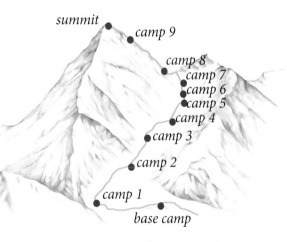

Here you can see the route to the summit of Mount Everest. Heavy equipment had to be carried from camp to camp.

It's Quiz Time!

The pages where you can find the answers are shown in the red circles, except where otherwise noted.

Extreme word search

F	L	E	R	Y	E	B	S	U	G	Q	I	G	T	
H	R	R	E	F	R	A	L	O	I	G	P	N	I	A
O	Q	U	E	N	C	E	C	I	E	O	E	R	W	G
A	N	T	A	R	C	T	I	C	Z	M	K	E	E	C
F	I	A	X	N	Y	C	T	C	N	Z	A	E	K	L
M	H	R	I	V	U	Y	C	O	A	T	A	Z	F	I
Q	L	E	O	U	O	C	R	O	H	L	C	R	V	M
Y	M	P	C	T	T	I	A	E	R	C	G	J	D	A
F	L	M	H	F	V	P	R	U	I	K	I	S	T	T
F	Z	E	G	N	N	M	K	P	V	O	M	R	V	E
C	J	T	E	T	H	G	U	O	R	D	E	I	L	A
H	U	M	I	D	H	H	F	I	X	S	H	A	C	V
B	G	E	H	Z	S	H	W	V	E	Q	K	D	M	E
Q	S	H	V	K	K	T	F	D	E	O	X	C	W	S
A	C	Z	H	S	B	E	L	G	S	U	F	L	C	V

Find these words in this extreme mix up of letters.

Antarctic
Arctic
blizzard
climate
desert
drought
environment
glacier
humid
ice
temperature
weather

Choose the correct word

1. The first people to reach the summit of Mount Everest were Edmund (Hillary, Hilarity, Hilary) and (Tennyson, Tamzin, Tenzing) Norgay. ⑲

2. Swamps are found in the tropics, close to the equator, in hot and (humid, humorous, hummus) environments. ⑤

3. Approximately four million (penguins, people, plants) live in the Arctic regions. ⑦

Complete these sentences

1. Glaciers begin to move downhill, under the force of _ _ _ _ _ _ _. ⑩

2. Volcanoes erupt when the _ _ _ _ inside our planet becomes too _ _ _ and melts to become magma. ⑪

3. Our _ _ _ _ _ _ _ is changing. ⑭

4. Temperatures in the depths of the _ _ _ _ _ are very, very _ _ _ _. ⑤

5. Deserts are _ _ _ regions, which usually receive less than 10 inches (25 cm) _ _ _ _ _ _ _ _ _ _ _ _ _ _ a year. ⑥

Answer:

21

Try It Out!

Reread the information about global warming and greenhouse gases on page 14. We are going to put those ideas into action.

What You'll Need:

- plastic sandwich bag, two thermometers, a sunny day

What to Do:

Place one thermometer in your plastic bag. Take both thermometers outside and leave them in a sunny spot for 15 minutes. Then read both thermometers. What happened? The one in the plastic bag should show a higher temperature. The plastic bag is like Earth's atmosphere. It holds the heat from the Sun inside.

Now Try This!

To see how a glacier changes Earth, balance a plastic plate on some books to make a hill. Put a line of candy sprinkles across the middle of the plate. Pour honey along the top of the plate. As the honey moves slowly downhill, it pulls some of the sprinkles down, too. This is the same way a glacier picks up and moves rocks and other matter.

Glossary

cirques (SURKS) Half-open steep-sided hollows at the head of a valley or on a mountainside formed by glacial erosion.

climate (KLY-mit) A long-term pattern of weather that characterizes a region.

climatologist (kly-muh-TO-luh-jist) A scientist who studies Earth's climate.

continent (KON-tuh-nent) One of the main masses of land in the world.

deforestation (dee-for-uh-STAY-shun) The loss of trees from an area.

fossil fuels (FO-sul FYOOLZ) Fuel, such as oil or coal, that comes from the remains of prehistoric animals or plants.

humid (HYOO-med) Having a relatively high level of water vapor in the atmosphere.

inundates (IH-nun-dayts) Floods.

latitudes (LA-tih-toodz) The distance of places from the equator, measured in degrees.

magma (MAG-muh) Hot, melted rock.

magnitude (MAG-nih-tood) Size or extent.

oceanographer (oh-shuh-NAH-gruh-fur) A scientist who studies the ocean and its inhabitants.

precipitation (preh-sih-pih-TAY-shun) Rain, sleet, snow or hail that falls to the ground.

spurs (SPERZ) Projections from mountains.

terrain (tuh-RAYN) The shape or features of the land surface.

tundra (TUN-druh) A treeless region bordering the Arctic.

windchill (WIND-chil) A measure expressing the lowering of the air temperature caused by the wind, affecting the rate of heat loss from the human body.

Index

A

altitude(s), 4, 19

Antarctica, 4, 7

Arctic, 4, 7

B

blizzard(s), 4, 9

C

climate(s), 4, 6, 14, 17

conditions, 4–5, 7

D

desert(s), 4, 6, 13

E

environment(s), 4–5, 7

I

ice storm(s), 4, 9

M

magma, 11

magnitude, 15

O

ocean(s), 4–5, 7, 13, 15–18

oxygen, 4

P

polar region(s), 4, 6–7

precipitation, 6

S

spurs, 10

T

temperature(s), 4–6, 9, 14, 19

terrain, 6

tundra, 5

W

windchill, 9

Web Sites

Due to the changing nature of Internet links, PowerKids Press has developed an online list of Web sites related to the subject of this book. This site is updated regularly. Please use this link to access the list:

www.powerkidslinks.com/ssm/grind/

24